DK

A DORLING KINDERSLEY BOOK

Designer Ingrid Mason
Illustrator Graham Corbett
Picture researcher Sue Wookey
Photography Peter Anderson, Jim Coit,
and Roland Kemp

First published in Canada in 1996 by
Stoddart Publishing Co. Limited,
34 Lesmill Road, Toronto, Canada M3B 2T6

First published in Great Britain in 1995
by Dorling Kindersley Limited
9 Henrietta Street, London WC2E 8PS

Canadian Cataloguing in Publication Data

Main entry under title:
The teddy bear counting book

ISBN 0-7737-2954-2

1. Counting - Juvenile literature. 2. Counting-out rhymes - Juvenile literature.
3. Picture books for children. I. Corbett, Grahame. II. Anderson, Peter, 1956-
III. Coit, Jim. IV. Title.

QA113.T43 1996   j513.2'11   C96-930124-3

Reproduced by Bright Arts, Hong Kong
Printed and bound in Italy by L.E.G.O.

1 2 3 4 5 6 7 8 9 10

The
Teddy Bear
Counting Book

Stoddart

1 2 3 4 5 6 7 8 9 10

1

One big bear,

2

Two make a pair.

3

Three all in brown,

4

Four go to town.

5

Five looking fluffy,

6

Six very scruffy.

Seven bears in bows,

8

Eight in two rows.

9

Nine making friends,

10

Ten, that's the end!